PIRATE

ATOMIC

MARC TYLER NOBLEMAN

Raintree

www.raintreepublishers.co.uk
Visit our website to find out more information about **Raintree** books.

To order:
☎ Phone 44 (0) 1865 888112
▤ Send a fax to 44 (0) 1865 314091
▢ Visit the Raintree bookshop at **www.raintreepublishers.co.uk** to browse our catalogue and order online.

First published in Great Britain by Raintree, Halley Court, Jordan Hill, Oxford OX2 8EJ, part of Harcourt Education. Raintree is a registered trademark of Harcourt Education Ltd.

Editorial: Louise Galpine and Harriet Milles
Design: Victoria Bevan, Steve Mead and Bigtop
Picture research: Mica Brancic
Illustrations: Jeff Edwards
Production: Julie Carter

Originated by Chroma Graphics Pte. Ltd
Printed and bound in China by Leo Paper Group

ISBN 978 1 4062 0676 0 (hardback)
12 11 10 09 08
10 9 8 7 6 5 4 3 2 1

ISBN 978 1 4062 0697 5 (paperback)
12 11 10 09 08
10 9 8 7 6 5 4 3 2 1

**British Library
Cataloguing in Publication Data**
Nobleman, Marc Tyler
Pirate. – (Atomic)
364.1'64
A full catalogue record for this book is available from the British Library.

Acknowledgements
The publishers would like to thank the following for permission to reproduce photographs: Corbis/Bettmann p. **5**; Getty Images pp. **6**, **18** (The Bridgeman Art Library), **17** (Photographer's Choice), p. **25** bottom (Hulton Archive), p. **25** top (Rischgitz), p. **29** (Michael Goldwater); Jasin Boland/The Kobal Collection/Universal p. **26**; Mary Evans Picture Library pp. **13**, **14**; Masterfile pp. **10** (Imtek Imagineering), p. **21** (G. Biss); The Bridgeman Art Library p. **22**; The Kobal Collection/Walt Disney Pictures p. **26**.

Cover photograph of a pirate reproduced with permission of Photolibrary/Mauritius Die Bildagentur Gmbh.

The publishers would like to thank Diana Bentley, Nancy Harris, and Dee Reid for their assistance in the preparation of this book.

Every effort has been made to contact copyright holders of any material reproduced in this book. Any omissions will be rectified in subsequent printings if notice is given to the publishers.

Contents

Some words are printed in bold, **like this**. You can find out what they mean in the glossary. You can also look in the box at the bottom of the page where the word first appears.

WHAT IS A PIRATE?

Far out at sea, the crew from one ship attacks the crew from another. They swing their swords and grab what they want. This is the pirate's way.

A pirate is a thief at sea. Pirates **plunder** other ships or go ashore to rob. Between 1680 and 1725, pirates stole more treasure and goods than ever. This period is called the **golden age** of piracy.

Who became pirates during the "golden age"?

Some sailors worked in the navy. They became pirates after a war ended and they needed a new job. Others were captured by pirates and forced to join. Some became pirates because they thought it would be exciting.

"Golden age" pirates often travelled in the Atlantic Ocean and the Caribbean Sea. The purple areas on this map show where they most liked to operate!

New York
Virginia
UNITED STATES
OF AMERICA
ATLANTIC
OCEAN
Gulf of Mexico
Bahamas
MEXICO
Cuba
Puerto Rico
Jamaica   Haiti
Caribbean Sea   Trinidad and
Tobago
SOUTH
AMERICA

0   1,000 miles
0   1,000 km

People from many different countries worked as pirates.

crew	people who work on a ship
golden age	most successful or famous time for a certain group
plunder	to steal. The word is also used to mean the items that are stolen.

Many pirates think of themselves as businessmen, not robbers.

ammunition	items such as bullets that are shot from weapons
privateer	pirate hired to steal for a nation

WHAT DO PIRATES DO?

Pirates steal money, jewellery, gold, and silver. They will also take anything they can sell. This can include food, alcohol, spices, ammunition, and even the ship itself!

Why do pirates steal?

Some pirates become wealthy very quickly.

Usually pirates steal to earn a living for themselves. In the past, some governments hired pirates called **privateers** to steal from enemy ships. The government and the privateers then split the **plunder**.

Some pirates only killed enemies if they resisted. They knew that if they killed too often, future enemies would fight back harder.

Pirate Fact!

Some privateers attacked ships of the country they worked for!

LIFE ON A PIRATE SHIP

A golden age pirate ship was more than just transport – it was also home to many men. Pirates worked, slept, and stored their loot there.

What did pirates eat at sea?

On board pirates ate turtle meat and biscuits called **hard tack**. The lack of fresh fruits and vegetables caused some pirates to get **scurvy**. It made their gums bleed.

Many pirates used small ships that could escape quickly. Yet such small ships could be cramped. Some ships had **crews** of a dozen or so men, while others held 80 or more.

hard tack	biscuit that does not spoil quickly
loot	stolen money or other items
scurvy	disease caused by a lack of the vitamin C found in fruits and vegetables
sloop	small ship that can sail into shallow water

Pirates often sailed on a
type of ship called a **sloop**.

Pirate Fact!

Some pirate ships had few
guns. Pirates often scared
enemies into surrendering
without firing a shot.

PIRATE'S ARTICLES (RULES)

✳ The Captain shall have the biggest share of all Prizes (plunder).

✳ If any man tries to run away, or steals or keeps secrets from the ship's **crew**, he will be shot or **marooned** with one bottle of gunpowder, one bottle of water, one small weapon, and a little **ammunition**.

✳ Any man who hits another man on board ship will be whipped 39 times on his bare back.

✳ Any man who smokes tobacco below deck (without a cap on his pipe), or carries a lighted candle without a cover, will be whipped.

✳ Lights must be out by 8:00 p.m.

✳ Any man who does not keep his weapons clean and ready to fight, or neglects his duties, will be punished as the Captain and the crew shall think fit.

Each captain had his own rules. Pirates had to agree to the rules by signing their names.

PIRATE RULES

Pirate captains wanted to keep their crews' behaviour under control. Their ships had "Articles", or rules. All on board had to agree to these rules.

Fierce but fair

Pirate crews made decisions as a group. They voted on who would be captain and which ships to attack. Everyone shared the **plunder**, though the captain got more.

To prevent fires, pirates could not smoke below deck and had to keep candles inside lanterns.

Because pirates could go into battle at any time, their guns always had to be clean and at the ready.

maroon	to leave a person on an island

PIRATE PUNISHMENTS

Pirate captains punished prisoners or even crew members who broke a rule. The punishments were often creative, and always painful.

How did pirates punish people?

Marooning was leaving a person on a small island by himself with no food and just a little water. **Keelhauling** was dragging a person under the ship by a rope. **Flogging** was beating a person with a whip.

How did the law punish pirates?

After naval sailors captured pirates, they brought them to shore for trial. Often pirates were hanged while townspeople watched.

Pirate Fact!

Sometimes the body of a hanged pirate was left in public for months. This reminded everyone what the law did to pirates.

This pirate has been marooned. Pirates were always at risk. Many thought they would not live long. They were usually right!

flog   to whip

keelhaul   to drag a person by rope under a ship

Pirate Fact!

Some pirates wore bandanas on their heads to keep sweat out of their eyes. Some also wore three-cornered hats.

How Pirates Looked

Up close, many pirates were scary – and smelly. They spent months at sea without bathing or changing their clothes regularly. Any teeth that had not fallen out were probably rotten.

Did all pirates look the same?

Pirates had no uniforms. They wore clothes that were comfortable for the difficult work on a ship.

Some pirate captains wore coats down to (and boots up to) their knees. Other pirates wore shorter coats and went barefoot on board ship.

According to some **historians**, pirates believed that wearing hoop earrings kept them from getting **seasick**.

bandana	cloth often worn around the head
historian	someone who studies history
seasick	feeling sick from the motion of a ship

Pirate Myths That Are True

Pirate life during the golden age was sometimes stranger than fiction.

The Jolly Roger is a flag with a picture of a skull and crossbones. Pirate ships flew flags like this to warn other ships. It meant that they were going to take prisoners. A red flag was more threatening. It meant pirates planned to kill anyone who tried to stop them.

Were there animals on board?

Pirates sold parrots, monkeys, and other exotic animals to wealthy people. Some pirates may have kept a parrot to amuse themselves at boring moments between robberies.

Sometimes pirates lost eyes or legs to **cutlasses** or cannonballs. Afterwards, some wore eye patches or used a wooden peg leg.

Pirate Fact!

Injured pirates were paid extra. They got more money for losing a right arm than a left.

Pirate ships flew flags like this Jolly Roger to warn other ships.

cutlass | short, curved sword often used by pirates

Real pirates did not usually force blindfolded enemies to **walk the plank**. It was easier just to throw people overboard!

Pirate Myths That Are False

Most pirate tales are wild, but not all are true.

Did pirates bury treasure?

Almost no **golden age** pirates buried treasure. They preferred to spend their **loot** on food, drink, and other pleasures.

The only known pirate who buried treasure was Captain Kidd. Some gold and silver that he buried in 1699 on an island near New York, USA has been dug up. People are still searching for the rest.

Pirate Fact!

Author Robert Louis Stevenson made up the famous pirate phrase "yo ho ho". No real pirate ever said that.

walk the plank to be forced to step off a board on a ship and then into the sea

PIRATE LINGO

Golden age pirates created a language all their own. Have you heard people say "Do you savvy?" "Savvy" is the pirate way to say "Do you understand?"

Have you heard these words?

"Sea dog" is another term for "pirate", especially a British pirate. A "landlubber" is a person who is clumsy on a ship. A "matey" is an assistant to the captain, although pirates sometimes used the word for other people.

"Ahoy" is similar to "hello". If a pirate yelled "avast", others would stop and pay attention. "Smartly" and "handsomely" were pirate words for "quickly". Honestly!

Pirate Fact!

19 September is International "Talk Like a Pirate Day". Arrr!

lingo	words used by a certain group, such as pirates

"Pieces of eight" means silver coins. "Doubloons" means gold coins. Stolen items were called "booty".

Bonny and Read were by far the fiercest fighters on Calico Jack's ship.

FEMALE PIRATES

In the golden age, female pirates were not common, although they did exist.

Anne Bonny and Mary Read are two of the best-known female pirates. By chance both ended up on the ship of the same pirate, Calico Jack.

What did male pirates think of Bonny and Read?

Each woman had dressed like a man to sneak aboard. The male pirates discovered the truth, but allowed them to stay. Bonny and Read fought too well to be kicked off!

Pirate Fact!

Bonny and Read were captured in the Caribbean Sea near Jamaica in 1720. Read died in prison soon after. What happened to Bonny is still a mystery.

WENTWORTH

FAMOUS PIRATES

Most of the pirates who became famous are the ones who got caught.

In 1718 Blackbeard was killed off the coast of North Carolina, USA. It took more than five gunshots and twenty **cutlass** wounds to finish him off. The man who killed Blackbeard hung the pirate's head from his ship.

Another pirate, Black Bart, was famous because he captured more than 400 ships. He was eventually killed by a cannon.

Were all pirates treated like villains?

Sir Henry Morgan was a **buccaneer**, meaning a pirate in the Caribbean Sea. He got rich and was honoured by the king of England.

buccaneer   pirate who worked in the Caribbean Sea

Henry Morgan was a favourite of Charles II, the king of England.

Before battles, Blackbeard stuck burning ropes into his hair to frighten enemies.

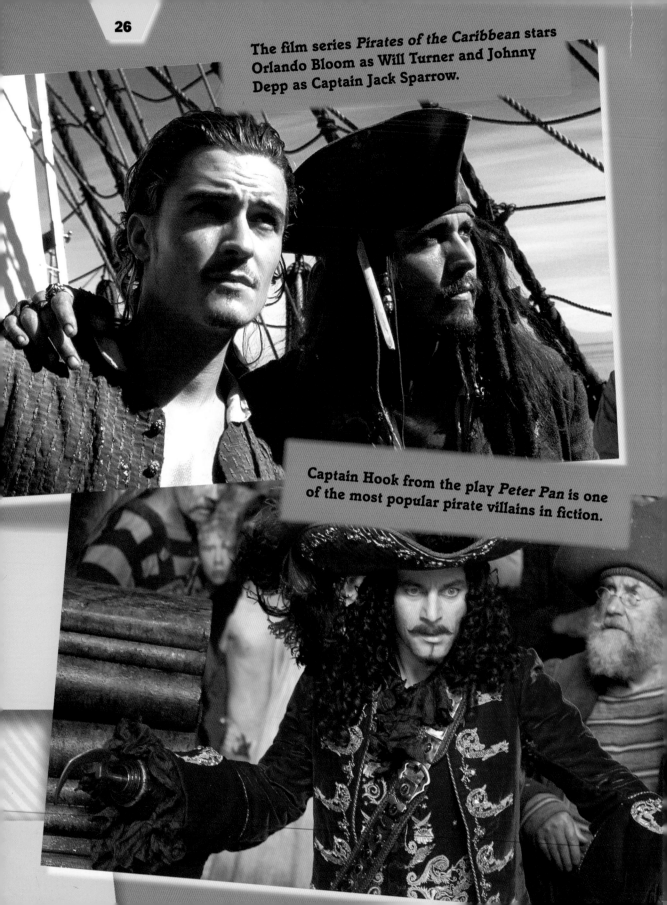

The film series *Pirates of the Caribbean* stars Orlando Bloom as Will Turner and Johnny Depp as Captain Jack Sparrow.

Captain Hook from the play *Peter Pan* is one of the most popular pirate villains in fiction.

Pirates In Popular Culture

Whether pirates are nasty or just naughty, people are fascinated by them. Pirates star in many popular stories.

As famous as real pirates

The novel *Treasure Island* by Robert Louis Stevenson came out in 1883. It features Long John Silver, a pirate with a parrot and a peg leg.

In the 1904 play *Peter Pan*, Captain Hook is a pirate with a hook for a hand.

Captain Jack Sparrow of the *Pirates of the Caribbean* films is more of a hero than a villain.

All these pirates are as famous as the real pirates.

Pirate Fact!

Today pirates are often sports mascots. The Pittsburgh Pirates are a baseball team in the USA.

MODERN PIRATES

Pirates are still a problem today around the world.

How do modern pirates steal?

Modern pirates drive speedboats. Sometimes pirates in several speedboats surround a ship. Other times pirates pretend their own boat is in trouble. When another ship stops to help, the pirates quickly board and **raid** it.

Sometimes modern pirates carry guns or knives and take passengers **hostage**. They ask a government to pay them **ransom** to free the hostages.

Modern pirates do not have eye patches or peg legs. Yet like pirates of the past, they are dangerous.

cargo	items for sale carried in large ships
hostage	person who is held prisoner against his or her will
raid	to search a place quickly and take what you want
ransom	money that kidnappers demand in exchange for freeing hostages

Modern pirates steal money, drugs, weapons, and more.

Areas where pirates operate today

ASIA

CHINA

South China Sea

PHILIPPINES

AFRICA

INDONESIA

ATLANTIC OCEAN

INDIAN OCEAN

0   3,000 miles

0   4,000 km

Modern pirates are most active in the South China Sea and near Africa. Many **cargo** ships sail there, carrying valuable loads.

Glossary

ammunition items such as bullets that are shot from weapons

bandana cloth often worn around the head

buccaneer pirate who worked in the Caribbean Sea

cargo items for sale carried in large ships

crew people who work on a ship

cutlass short, curved sword often used by pirates

flog to whip a person or animal

golden age most successful or famous time for a certain group

hard tack biscuit that does not spoil quickly

historian someone who studies history

hostage person who is held prisoner against his or her will

keelhaul to drag a person by rope under a ship

lingo words used by a certain group, such as pirates

loot stolen money or other items

maroon to leave a person on an island

plunder to steal. The word is also used to mean the items that are stolen.

privateer pirate hired to steal for a nation

raid to search a place quickly and take what you want

ransom money that kidnappers demand in exchange for freeing hostages

scurvy disease caused by a lack of the vitamin C found in fruits and vegetables

seasick feeling sick from the motion of a ship

sloop small ship that can sail into shallow water

walk the plank to be forced to step off a board on a ship and then into the sea

Want to Know More?

Books

✳ *On the Edge: Pirates*, Christopher Richardson (Chelsea House, 2005)

✳ *Piracy and Plunder: A Murderous Business*, Milton Meltzer (Dutton, 2001)

✳ *Pirates*, John Matthews (Atheneum, 2006)

✳ *Pirates and Smugglers*, Moira Butterfield (Kingfisher, 2005)

Websites

✳ www.nationalgeographic.com/ pirates/bbeard.html
Find out more about Blackbeard.

✳ people.howstuffworks.com/ pirate.html
Learn more about pirates.

✳ blindkat.hegewisch.net/pirates/ jolirouge.html
Take a look at pirate flags.

If you liked this Atomic book, why don't you try these...?

Index

Notes for adults

Use the following questions to guide children towards identifying features of explanation text:

Can you find an example of a main heading and side heading on page 4?
Can you find the different ways that pirates were punished on page 12?
Can you give examples of two connectives from page 16?
Can you find two examples of the present tense on page 20?
Can you give examples of side headings starting with 'how', 'why', and 'what'?